DIET
My Arse!

DIET
My Arse!

CATHY HAMILTON

EBURY
PRESS

First published in USA by Andrews McMeel Publishing, an Andrews
McMeel Universal company, 4520 Main Street,
Kansas City, Missouri 64111

This edition first published in Great Britain in 2001
Ebury Press
Random House
20 Vauxhall Bridge Road
London SW1 2SA

10 9 8 7 6 5

Random House Australia (Pty) Limited
20 Alfred Street, Milsons Point, Sydney,
New South Wales 2061, Australia

Random House New Zealand Limited
18 Poland Road, Glenfield,
Auckland 10, New Zealand

Random House (Pty) Limited
Endulini, 5a Jubilee Road, Parktown 2193, South Africa

The Random House Group Limited Reg. No. 954009

www.randomhouse.co.uk

ISBN 0 09 1884004

A CIP catalogue record for this book
is available from the British Library

Papers used by Ebury Press are natural, recyclable products
made from wood grown in sustainable forests.

Typeset by Aniz Damani
Cover design by the Senate
Front cover and interior image © Photonica
Printed and bound in Denmark by Nørhaven Paperback, Viborg

CONTENTS

—♀—

RULES

AND

RATIONALI-
ZATIONS

☿

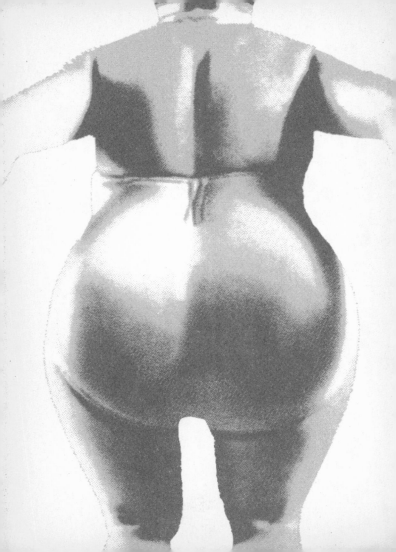

If you *think* you're big-boned, you *are* big-boned.

N
ever ask a man
"Do I look fat?"
as if you expect an honest
answer.

No man has the right to know
how much you weigh,
except your physician and
lifeboat captain.

*This includes boyfriends
and husbands.*

When a fellow girl asks
"Do I look fat?" the best
answer is "You look great!"

If you think your metabolism
is slow, it *is* slow.

It is never appropriate to make the comment "I am so fat!" if:

You are a size 10 or smaller.
You are the exact same size
  or smaller than any girl in
  the room.

You are a Victoria's Secret
  model or someone with
  similar proportions.

You used to be fat but have
  recently lost a significant
  amount of weight.

N ever, *ever* ask a woman "When are you due?" unless you're *sure* she's pregnant!

Author's note:
Once, while wearing a baggy jumper, I was asked this question by an acquaintance of my mother's. When I explained that I was not, in fact, pregnant, the woman was mortified. Her face turned the color of paprika and she apologized no less than nine times. Her attempts at atonement were worse than the original remark, which is why I also recommend . . .

10

If someone asks you
"When are you due?" and
you are *not*, in fact, pregnant,
simply reply:
"Any minute now!"
Save yourself
the aggravation.

You are *not* what you eat.

*How ridiculous is that?
I mean, if that were true, we'd
all be nothing but big vats of
spaghetti carbonara.*

You can reasonably attribute
five pounds of your weight
at any given time to
"water retention."

*Before your period, ten to fifteen
pounds is acceptable.*

You may understate your weight by up to twenty-five pounds without raising an eyebrow.

Any more and you're pushing your luck.

A woman is never expected
to tell the truth about
her weight.

Never ask another woman
"How much do you weigh?"
unless you are a doctor,
nurse, anesthesiologist,
or lifeboat captain.

If you hang out with fatter people, you will look thinner.

This is particularly true by the pool or on the beach.

(Warning: Hanging out with the fatties too often could give you a false sense of security and lead to overeating.)

17

Never date a man with thinner arms than yours.

Author's note:
My rule used to be "never date a man with thinner thighs than yours" until I realized I had eliminated 90 percent of the eligible men in the free world.

Keep plenty of healthy
snacks around the house
and office.

*Even if you never touch them,
you'll give others the impression
that you're trying.*

19

THE
BUDDY
SYSTEM

♀

It is never acceptable to sabotage a fellow girl's diet, even if you desperately want someone to binge with.

It's a given that when you lose weight, others will be jealous and try to sabotage you.

Note: These people are not your true friends.

When a girl tells you how much weight she's lost, don't question the amount. Believe her and cheer for every pound.

When you know a girl has
been dieting seriously for more
than two weeks, tell her she
looks skinnier . . . even if
she doesn't!

When a fellow girl has lost a
significant amount of weight,
applaud her efforts like
you'd want her to celebrate
with you.

When a girlfriend is dieting, don't eat ice cream, chocolate, or other tempting foods in front of her.

But if you must (say, like at a wedding), don't act like you're enjoying it. Tell her it's the worst cake you ever had.

When you are on a diet, you are not required to cook a separate meal for the nondieting members of your household.

Let the skinny freaks fend for themselves.

It is never advisable to start
a weight-loss competition
with a girlfriend.

It's a no-win situation.
No matter which one of you loses
more, the other will lose less.
So you both lose.

N ever *ever* compete in a
weight-loss contest
with a man.

*Men can lose ten pounds in three
days just by giving up beer. Dieting
is aggravating enough . . . who
needs that?*

There is nothing more
obnoxious than a person
who has lost a significant
amount of weight and thinks
she has suddenly become
the calorie police.

If you're going to cheat,
go all the way.

*Don't waste a perfectly good binge
on something stupid like a
custard cream biscuit when, for the
same amount of guilt, a crème
brûlée is MUCH more satisfying.*

THE
BOTTOM
LINE

♀

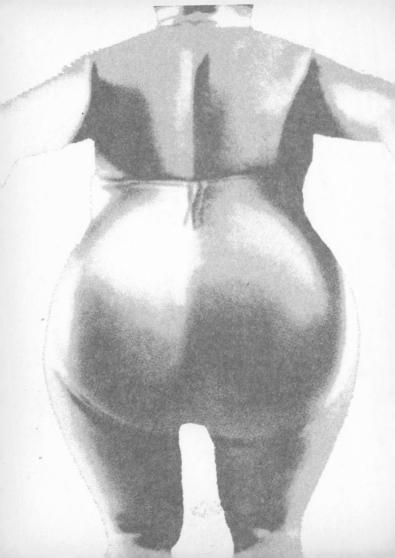

N ever ask a man
"Does my butt look big?"
and expect an answer you
can live with.

Visible panty lines add
ten pounds.

Avoid them at all costs.

Friends don't let friends wear bum bags.

Hipster jeans were designed for women with no hips.

Only one out of 99 women
can get away with wearing
a thong.

*Chances are, you're not
one of them.*

SHOPPING
STRATEGIES

♀

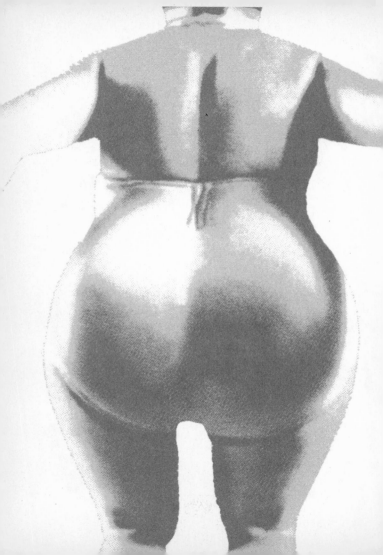

When shopping for swimsuits,
always go solo.

Never shop with girls who are significantly skinnier than you. A good rule of thumb is to practice departmental segregation.

Juniors should not shop with
Teens.

Teens should not shop with
Women's.

Petites should not shop with
Talls, etc.

If someone asks what size
you are, it is appropriate to
answer with the lowest size
in your closet that you can still
squeeze into.

If a girl asks you if an outfit makes her look fat, tell her the truth gently. Say "I think you could find something more flattering," or "It doesn't seem to hang very well on you."

You'd want her to do the same for you.

Never tell a fellow girl that something doesn't look good on her, then turn around and buy it for yourself.

Designer clothes almost
always run larger than
knock-offs.

*Sometimes, it's worth spending the
extra money to say you
wear a 10.*

When in doubt,
buy the larger size.

*This is especially true
for swimsuits.*

The outfit will never look as fabulous on you as it does on the mannequin.

Keep in mind, the typical model is over five foot ten tall and measures 34-24-35.

Tube tops, bicycle shorts, white jeans, and thongs were never meant to be worn by normal-sized women.

Department store sales clerks
are never to be trusted.

*Have you ever known one to
say "Honey, that outfit makes you
look hippy. Why don't
you try the store across
the mall?"*

55

Shoulder pads never have
to go out of style.

Lycra is your friend.

BINGE
BYLAWS

♀

If a girlfriend goes on a binge after a bad break-up, you have a moral obligation to join her.

If the break-up wasn't her
doing, you are obliged to spring
for the ice cream
and the booze.

It is permissible to
break a diet when:

There's been a divorce or
   break-up.

You've been fired.

You've been promoted.

You've paid your rent on time.

Your parents are in town.

Your boyfriend is out of town.

It's Saturday night and you
   don't have a date.

It's a three-day weekend.

You're dining at a four-star restaurant or above.

You've stuck to the diet for four weeks.

It's Valentine's Day or any other chocolate-oriented holiday.

There's a sale on Ben and Jerry's or Sara Lee.

If you eat standing up, the
calories don't count.

*This rule also applies to anything
eaten on your birthday.*

If you are on a business trip with a £50-a-day meal allowance, you may deduct up to £50 worth of calories per diem, excluding liquor.

Likewise, food purchased with a 15 percent off coupon has 15 percent fewer calories.

Silly or improbable food,
like cheesy balls,
has no calories.

*Because who takes food like that
seriously anyway?*

66

Foods used for medicinal or therapeutic purposes, such as cough drops, hot cocoa, toast, soup and crackers, pizza, or hot fudge sundaes, *don't count.*

Food from the children's menu has 40 percent fewer calories than the same food on the regular menu because it costs 40 percent less.

Food that you eat off other people's plates, especially children's, has no calories. It is "borrowed" food and can thus be "returned."

This is why you can finish your kids' desserts every night without gaining a pound.

Food eaten in total darkness
doesn't count.

Eat slowly.

If you can make lunch last eight hours, you won't need dinner.

Broken cookie pieces, brownie
crumbs, and slivers
of cheesecake contain
no calories.

Foods licked off knives, spatulas, or mixer blades have no calories if you are in the act of preparing or cooking food.

The energy you expend while making the food negates any calories contained in the licked portions.

Calorie counts are listed "per serving," meaning from the finished dish; they do not include ingredients while the dish is being prepared.

Likewise, cookie dough and cake batter have no calories until they are baked.

So lick all you want.

F̲ood eaten on the run—
in the car or on foot—
has no calories.

*"On the run" is the equivalent
of "running," which burns up to
eight hundred calories per hour
(depending on your weight),
thus negating your intake and
accelerating your metabolism
for the rest of the day.*

76

Hot food that gets cold loses
its calories, and they will not
be regained when it is reheated
if a microwave
is used.

If you are eating food sold to you by nonprofit organizations such as the Girl Scouts, Brownies or the Church Roof Appeal, you may deduct 50 percent of the calories as a charitable donation.

If you are eating food at any event which promotes World Peace (this includes Neighbourhood Watch meetings) it should be regarded as calorie free.

THE NAKED
TRUTH
(OR FULL
DISCLOTHESURE)

♀

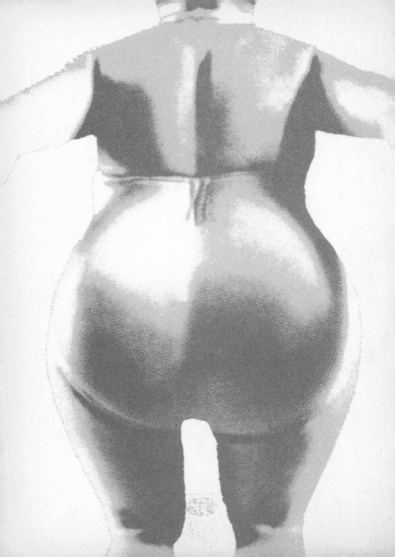

Every girl has the right to get dressed in private.

Y ou are never required to
stand naked in front of anyone.
This includes husbands,
boyfriends,
and doctors.

*Exception: Prison guards, which
should be all the motivation
you need to stay out of jail.*

A naked body looks ten pounds slimmer in the dark.

Subtract five pounds if you are on your back.

Subtract another ten if you are under the covers.

A tanned body looks ten
pounds slimmer than
a pale body.

Never put on a pair of
panty hose in front of anyone
you're trying to impress.

EXERCISING
YOUR
RIGHTS

♀

Sitting is *too* an exercise.

*Done properly, it can burn up
to thirty calories per hour.*

Exercise performed for any charitable cause such as marathons, walkathons, or swimathons burns twice as many calories—one set for you and one for the cause.

Always work out next to
people who are in worse
shape than you.

You may not interrupt
a fellow girl's workout just
because you are gasping
for breath and need a
bagel break.

If you feel faint at any point during exercise - EAT.

You may be ill and losing weight by the minute. Chocolate isn't there for pleasure. It's there to keep your strength up.

MIRRORS, SCALES, AND OTHER DISTORTIONS OF NATURE

♀

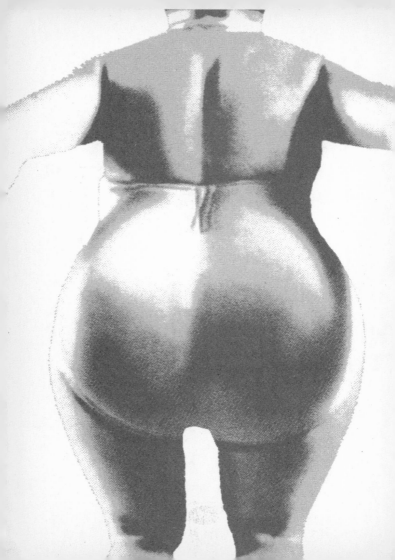

Weigh yourself once a week—
before the weekend,
not after.

Don't even think about
stepping on a scale when you're
suffering from PMS.

*What are you, a glutton
for punishment?*

When your weight fluctuates
from one scale to another, even
by five pounds or more, the
lighter scale is *always*
the accurate one.

*This is especially important to
remember in the gym and at
Weight Watchers meetings.*

Doctor's office scales always weigh you ten pounds heavier than your real weight.

Department store mirrors
always make you look
ten pounds skinnier
than your mirrors at home.

The camera adds ten pounds.

Fifteen pounds on the beach.

Never permit anyone to
take your photo from
below chin level.

Never allow anyone to take your photo while you're eating, drinking, squatting, bending over, playing Limbo or Twister, dancing, or jumping into a pool.

You may be a few pounds overweight but you've still got your dignity.